Handyman's

The Ultimate Collectic

Published by Glowworm Press
7 Nuffield Way
Abingdon OX14 1RL
By Chester Croker

Jokes for Handymen

These jokes for handymen will make you giggle. Some of these jokes are old, some of them are new and we hope you enjoy our collection of the very best handyman jokes and puns around.

You will find a mixture of stories and quick fire gags all written to make you laugh. Overall, this huge collection of handymen jokes is guaranteed to get you laughing.

FOREWORD

When I was asked to write a foreword to this book I was chuffed.

That is until I was told that I was the last resort by the author, Chester Croker, and that everyone else he had approached had said they couldn't do it!

I have known Chester for a number of years and his ability to create funny jokes is absolutely incredible. He is quick witted and an expert at crafting amusing puns.

He will be glad you have bought this book, as he has an expensive lifestyle to maintain.

Enjoy!

Jack Hammer

Table of Contents

Chapter 1: Handyman Jokes

If you're looking for handyman jokes you've certainly come to the right place.

In this book you will find corny and cheesy jokes that will hopefully make you laugh. Some of these handyman jokes are old, some of them are new, and we hope you enjoy our collection of the very best handyman jokes and puns around.

We've got some great one liners to start with, plenty of quick fire question and answer themed gags, some story led jokes and as a bonus some corny and cheesy handymen pick-up lines.

This mixture of jokes is guaranteed to get you laughing.

Chapter 2: One Liner Handyman Jokes

Duct tape is like the force. There is a light side and a dark side and it holds the universe together.

People call me a handyman. Well, I am good at building walls around me.

My first week on the "build it yourself" course went well. I think I nailed it.

I got called pretty the other day. Actually, the full sentence was "You're a pretty bad handyman." but I'm choosing to focus on the positives.

My wife is a real DIY fan.

Whenever I ask her to do something, she says "Do it yourself."

Did you hear about the handyman who had too many drinks? He was hammered.

Did you know that Hitler trained to be a carpenter? He even published a book "Mein Kampfy Chair". It wasn't successful though- he had a thing against screws.

My handyman business will slowly and surely take over all sorts of local trades until it gets to carpentry, then suddenly lots of carpenters will start coming out of the wood work.

Have you seen the joke that is doing the rounds on various forums about the handyman that had to re-do a fence that got messed up? I think it has been reposted a lot.

I think my dog wants to be a roofer. He likes roofing.

Sign seen on a van: Miller's Handyman Services. We will repair what your husband supposedly fixed.

Did you hear about the handyman who stole a calendar? He got twelve months.

I once thought about becoming a carpenter, but I didn't think it wood work. Then I thought about being a welder, but I soon realized that steel wooden work.

A handyman friend of mine gave me some great advice, saying I should put something away for a rainy day. I've gone for an umbrella.

If a handyman says he will fix it, he will. There's no need to remind him every six months.

My local handyman refused to make me a kitchen worktop. He said it would be counter-productive.

I just completed my carpentry exam. I got B+ for planning, A for sawing and A for hammering. I nailed it.

I went to a TV repairman's wedding recently. I have to say the reception was great.

I'm going to start a handyman business that employs illegal immigrants. I'm going to call it Manuel Labor.

My practical carpentry exam went really well. I totally nailed it.

A woman in my last job was a handyman's wet dream. Flat as a board and easy to nail.

I had to explain what irony was to someone at our church meeting today. Apparently "Being a carpenter and getting nailed to a wooden cross" wasn't a good example.

As a female handyman, I regularly get asked if I prefer to get screwed or nailed.

Last week I asked a handyman to do some odd jobs for me - I gave him a list of ten jobs, but he only did jobs 1,3,5,7 and 9.

Did you hear about the miracle of the blind handyman? He picked up a hammer and saw.

Did you hear about the Chinese lift repairman? It was Wong on so many levels.

Did you hear about the cross-eyed handyman who was sacked because he couldn't see eye to eye with his customers.

Living through a home renovation is like living in the wild -you will do whatever it takes to survive.

Did you hear about the drunken handyman? I heard he was hammered.

The inexperienced handyman screws things up, but the experienced handyman nails it.

I am learning to tap dance. Unfortunately, I'm not very good - I keep falling in the sink.

I am told I am a Jack of all trades, and a master of pun.

Yesterday, a handyman's wife asked him to pass her lipstick but he passed her a super-glue stick instead by mistake. She still isn't talking to him.

I suspected my friend of using my tools without my permission. When he boasted he had made a new front door decoration, I knew it was a sign.

A handyman wanted to buy something for his mother-in-law, so he bought her a new chair. She won't let him plug it in though.

When I was a carpenter, my marriage failed. My wife accused me of being a mahoganist.

Chapter 3: Question and Answer Handyman Jokes

Q: How many women does it take to change a light bulb?

A: As many as they need to pay the handyman.

Q: Which breakfast gurus would you ask for handyman advice?

A: The saw sages.

Q: Why does a handyman make a bad boyfriend?

A: He nuts and bolts.

Q: What was the name of the popular DIY store in Little Rock?

A: Ark-n-saw.

Q: How did the handyman know the board was cut in half?

A: He saw it.

Q: Why is a carpenter the easiest guy to get a Christmas gift for?

A: All they want for Christmas is Yew.

Q: A carpenter, a plumber, an electrician and a welder are all dating the same woman. What do you call her?

A: A jack off all trades.

Q: What do handymen and webcam girls have in common?

A: They both bang their fingers to make a living.

Q: Why did the handyman's wife leave him?

A: He was screwing around when he was supposed to be nailing her.

Q: What does a handyman do after a one night stand?

A: He makes a matching one for the other side of the bed.

Q: What did the carpenter say to the car painter?

A: You sound just like me.

Q: What does a handyman like about laying carpets?

A: He likes it when the carpets match the drapes.

Q: What happened to the door after the handyman said it was being replaced?

A: It got annoyed and became unhinged.

Q: Why did Jesus quit being a carpenter?

A: He got too attached to his work.

Q: How does a handyman build a set of stairs efficiently?

A: By thinking one step ahead.

Q: What does a handyman like about carpentry?

A: He can put his wood where he likes, and get paid for it.

Q: What do you do when your chair breaks?

A: Call a chairman.

Q: What did the handyman do when he got a horny girl into bed with him for the first time?

A: He screwed, nutted, and bolted.

Q: Why did the handyman join the army?

A: Because he wanted to become a Drill Sergeant.

Q: What was a handyman's prototype of a bar seat called?

A: A stool sample.

Chapter 4: Short Handyman Jokes

A woman asked me to look at her broken clock to see if I could fix it.

She told me, "The clock just goes tick, tick, tick." but I told her, "Don't worry; we have ways to make it tock."

Two handymen are nailing up a siding on a roof when the first handyman took a nail from his pouch, examined it, and then tossed it away.

He took another nail, examined it, and then hammered it into the siding.

He repeated this a few times, before his co-worker asked, "Why are you doing that?" to which the first handyman replied, "Well, half of these nails have the head on the wrong end."

The other handyman told him off saying, "You fool. Those are for the other side of the house."

I was chatting to my buddy who is a keen DIY-er who told me how he had tiled a huge bathroom and he was very pleased with the result, especially as it was the first time he had taken on a tiling project.

I asked how he learnt how to do it, and he told me that he mostly learned by tile and error.

I called my usual handyman to complain about my faulty ice making machine that had been leaking.

When he came back out to the house, he discovered it was just some ice that had fallen off the back and melted on the floor.

I apologized and the handyman told me not to worry, because as far as he was concerned, it was all water under the fridge.

A dozy DIY enthusiast takes his front door to his handyman friend and says, "Can you fix my front door for me?"

The handyman replies, "Sure, but what about your house, what if a burglar was to get in?"

The dozy guy replies, "Impossible. How could he get in when I've got the door right here with me?"

Here is the only knock knock joke in this book. It might take a couple of goes at reading it to get it!

Knock, knock.

Who's there?

Ding Dong.

Ding dong who?

Yes, I have fixed your doorbell.

My wife and I once had a lovely weekend away at a village in the countryside and we became friendly with the local handyman who told us that his neighbor had a pretty little cottage for sale.

Despite the cottage looking a little neglected, we fell in love with it and bought it.

When we moved in, our handyman friend came to welcome us and said, "You got a great deal, but it does need some work – the plumbing is awful, the wiring is dangerous and the roof leaks."

Dismayed, I said to him, "Why on earth didn't you tell us that before we bought it?" to which he replied "We weren't neighbors then."

A handyman in my area went to jail for dealing drugs.

I've been one of his customers for over five years, and I had no clue he was a handyman.

A handyman meets up with his blonde girlfriend as she is picking up her car from the mechanic.

He asks her, "Everything ok with your car now?"

"Yes, thank goodness," the blonde replies.

The handyman asks the blonde, "Weren't you worried the mechanic might try to rip you off?"

The blonde replies, "Yes I was, but he was good. He just said I needed was blinker fluid!"

My buddy is useless at DIY and rather slow at the best of times.

For a very small project the other day, he was going to use a screw, but I explained to him when to use a screw and when a nail, and for this project I recommended using nails.

He said to me, "What you're telling me is that I have to strike this thing repeatedly with a hammer?" to which I replied, "Yes, you hit the nail on the head."

The wealthy homeowner was delighted with the way the handyman had done all the work on his house.

"You did a great job." he said and handed the man his money as agreed. "Also, in order to thank-you, here's an extra 100 dollars to take the missus out to dinner."

Later that night, the doorbell rang and it was the handyman. The homeowner asked, "What's the matter, did you forget something?"

"Nope." replied the handyman, "I'm just here to take your missus out to dinner like you asked."

The handyman grumbled to his friend that his wife didn't satisfy him anymore.

His friend advised he find another woman on the side, pretty quick.

When they met up a month or so later, the handyman told his friend, "I took your advice and managed to find a woman on the side, yet my wife still doesn't satisfy me!"

We had our garage door repaired yesterday by a local handyman.

He told us that the main problems was that we did not have a large enough motor on the door opener.

I told him it was a 1/2 horsepower motor, and he said we needed a 1/4 horsepower motor.

I said that can't be right —and that 1/2 was larger than 1/4 and he said, "Oh no, Four is twice as large as two."

A handyman was working on fixing my garage doors.

I had just finished washing the floor when he asked me if he could use the toilet.

With dismay I looked at his muddy boots and my newly polished floor.

"Just a minute," I said, "I'll put down some newspaper."

"That's all right, madam" he said. "I'm house trained."

It was our first home do it up ourselves project and we worked really long hours painting and wallpapering and we were absolutely exhausted when we got into bed.

My husband was dozing away when I said to him, "Honey, did you notice that the moon is almost full."

He replied, through his slumber, "I'm really tired but don't worry; I'll empty it in the morning."

A handyman calls up his local newspaper and asks, "How much would it be to put an ad in your paper?"

"Three dollars an inch," a woman replies. "Why? What are you selling?"

"A twelve foot ladder," said the handyman before putting the phone down.

A handyman is struggling to find a parking space at his local Home Depot.

"Lord," he prayed. "I can't stand this. If you open a space up for me, I swear I'll give up the booze and go to church every Sunday."

Suddenly, the clouds part and the sun shines on an empty parking spot.

Without hesitation, the handyman says, "Never mind Lord, I found one."

I helped out a handyman friend of mine the other day who wanted to lay a new carpet in his den.

We laid out the bright purple carpet roll on the lawn so he could measure it properly and cut it to size.

The nosy next door neighbor popped her head over the fence and said if she had any say it, she would prefer we kept the lawn its normal color!

A handyman tries to enter a bar wearing a shirt that is open at the collar, and is met by a bouncer who tells him that he must wear a necktie to gain admission.

The handyman goes to his car as he knows he has some jump leads in his boot; and he makes some sort of knot and he lets the cable ends dangle free.

He goes back to the bar and the bouncer carefully looks him over, and then says, "OK, you can come in, but just don't try and start anything."

A dog walks into a pub, and takes a seat. He says to the barman, "I would like a large cold beer please."

The barman says, "Crikey, that's amazing; you should think about joining the circus.'"

The talking dog replies, "Why? Do they need handymen?"

A proud father is showing pictures of his three sons to an old work colleague and he is asked, "What do your boys do for a living?"

He replied, "Well my youngest is an attorney and my middle son is a surgeon."

"What does the oldest child do?" his friend asked.

The reply came, "He's the handyman that paid for the others' education."

A handyman goes to the doctor with a hearing problem.

The doctor says, "Can you describe the symptoms to me?"

The handyman replies, "Yes. Homer is a big fat yellow lazy man and Marge is tall with big blue hair."

A handyman was caught trading without a license, and his work was considered sub-standard.

In the court the judge received a note from his assistant and immediately declared him guilty for both working without a license and for perjury.

It turned out he had done some jury rigging.

A handyman took his cross-eyed Labrador to the vet.

The vet picked the dog up to examine him and said, "Sorry, I'm going to have to put him down."

The handyman said, "Oh, it's not that bad is it?"

The vet replied, "No, he's just very heavy."

Chapter 5: Longer Handyman Jokes

The Climbing Frame

A proud father brought home a swing and climbing frame set he had bought for his children and immediately began to try and assemble it while his kids were eagerly waiting to play on it.

After several hours of reading the assembly instructions and trying to fit bolt G into sub-slot H and so on, he gave up and asked an old handyman who was working in a neighboring yard to help.

The old-timer threw the installation instructions away, and he successfully assembled the climbing frame set in a very short period of time.

The pleased father asked him, "How did you manage to get it all put together without even reading the instructions?"

"Well, to tell the truth," replied the old-timer, "I can't read, and when you can't read, you've simply got to think."

Sushi Insulation

You might not be able to tell by looking at me, but I'm not a handyman. I'm not a DIY guy at all.

I'm the kind of person that looks at some rolled up pink fiberglass insulation and thinks that it looks like a big piece of sushi.

I only know to call it "Fiberglass insulation" because I once worked alongside my handyman father-in-law.

Imagine my surprise while we were refurbishing my house, he told me that I hammer like lightning.

I was quite pumped until he told me that lightning never hits the same spot twice.

The Phone Problem

A farmer called his handyman buddy to have a look at his weird phone problem – which mostly failed to ring when customers or friends called - and that when it did ring, his dog always howled just before the phone rang.

The handyman came to look at the problem and to see if the dog was psychic.

The handyman did some tests and found:-

1. The dog was tied to the telephone system's ground wire with a steel chain and collar.

2. The wire connection to the ground earthing rod was loose.

3. The dog received 90 volts of signaling current every time the farm's phone number was called.

4. After a couple of jolts, the dog would start crying and he would then urinate.

5. The wet ground would complete the circuit, thus causing the phone to ring.

The handyman thus demonstrated that some problems can be fixed by pissing and crying.

Train Passengers

A handyman, a lawyer, a beautiful lady, and an old woman were on a train, sitting 2x2 facing each other.

The train went into a tunnel and when the carriage went completely dark, a loud "smack" was heard.

When the train came out of the tunnel back into the light the lawyer had a red hand print on his face. He had been slapped on the face.

The old lady thought, "That lawyer must have groped the young lady in the dark and she slapped him."

The hottie thought, "That lawyer must have tried to grope me, got the old lady by mistake, and she slapped him."

The lawyer thought, "That handyman must have groped the hottie, she thought it was me, and slapped me."

The handyman just sat there thinking, "I can't wait for another tunnel so I can slap that lawyer again!"

A Sincere Apology

A man is at work one day, and he receives an email from his neighbor.

He opens it to read, "Dear neighbor. I must apologize for taking advantage of your wife. I have been doing it every day for many months now, and I've only recently been caught by the internet repairman, who noticed I was doing something unusual as he went into your house for his repair work. He has left now, and I'm afraid I no longer have access. I want to apologize, though, as I feel really guilty over my usage levels. Please forgive me."

The man went home immediately, and in a fit of rage, murdered his wife.

He sat down at his computer to search how to dispose of her body, when a new email from his neighbor popped up.

It said, "Dear neighbor, my apologies again but my autocomplete messed up on my last email. I meant Wi-Fi, not wife. I have been using your Wi-Fi, not your wife!"

Golf With A Priest

A handyman and a priest were playing a round of golf together.

The handyman swings, and misses. He yells out, "God damn it; I missed."

The priest rebukes him saying, "Thou shalt not take the name of thy Lord in vain."

The handyman swings once more and misses again and yells out, "God damn it; I missed."

The priest exclaims, "Be careful, the Lord might strike you down with lightning for that."

The handyman laughs him off and swings and misses again and shouts, "God damn it; I missed."

Suddenly, a bolt of lightning comes down from the sky and hits the priest who disappears in a puff of smoke.

A deep, booming voice is heard from above, "God damn it; I missed."

Painting The Porch

A cute blonde, wanting to earn some money, decided to hire herself out as a handywoman-type and started canvassing a wealthy neighborhood.

She went to the front door of a house and asked the owner if he had any jobs for her to do.

The owner replied, "Well, you can paint my porch. How much will you charge?"

The blonde said, "How about 100 dollars?"

The man agreed and told her that the paint and brushes that she would need were in the garage.

The man's wife, who was inside the house, overheard the conversation and asked her husband, "Does she realize that the porch goes all the way around the house?"

The man replied, "She must do. After all, she was standing on the porch."

A little while later, the blonde came to the door to collect her money.

"You're finished already?" he asked.

"Yes," the blonde answered, "and I had some paint left over, so I gave it two coats. Impressed, the man handed her $100.

By the way," the blonde added, "It's a Ferrari, not a Porch."

Washing Machine Repair

A handyman gets called out to fix a washing machine. He duly notes down the make and model number and then gives it a solid whack on the side. Instantly the machine starts to work again, and the handyman asks for 100 dollars.

The customer balks at the bill and says, "100 bucks? There's no way I'm going to pay you unless you can justify charging me 100 dollars for just smacking the side of the machine."

The handyman takes back the bill and re-writes it.

Services Rendered:

Whacking the washing machine $20

Knowing where to whack it $80

Three Friends

Ron is talking to two of his friends, Jim and Shamus.

Jim says, "I think my wife is having an affair with a handyman. The other day I came home and found a monkey wrench under our bed and it wasn't mine."

Shamus then confides, "Wow, me too! I think my wife is having an affair with an electrician. The other day I found wire cutters under the bed and they weren't mine."

Ron thinks for a minute and then says, "You know - I think my wife is having an affair with a horse."

Both Jim and Shamus look at him in complete disbelief.

Ron sees them looking at him and says, "No, seriously. The other day I came home early and found a jockey under our bed."

A Big Complainer

Last week I came home from a hard day at work, only to be moaned at by my wife. She says that the stairs are creaking and that I should fix it.

I tell her, "Do I look like a handyman?" and she walks out of the room.

The next day I get home from an exhausting day at work and my wife is moaning again, this time telling me the toilet doesn't flush anymore.

I say, "Do I look like a plumber?" and she leaves me in peace.

The next day I get home from a long day at work and she is moaning again. She says the walls in the main room are looking tired, and need painting.

I tell her, "Do I look like a painter?" and she walks away.

The next day I come home from work late, and I notice the stairs have been fixed, the toilet flushes and the walls have been freshly painted.

I say, "How did this happen?"

She said the handyman down the road did it all.

I say, "How much did it cost?"

She said she could have either baked him a cake, or given him a good time.

I asked her, "What kind of cake did you bake?"

She tells me, "Do I look like a baker?"

Bar Chat

A young handyman is sitting down at the bar having a drink after a hard day's graft, when a large, burly sweaty construction worker sits down next to him.

They strike up a conversation, and have a few beers together.

In due course they start talking about the prospect of nuclear war.

The handyman asks the construction worker, "If you heard the sirens go off, and you knew the missiles were on their way, and you know you've just 20 minutes or so left to live, what would you do?"

The construction worker replies, "I am going to grab anything that moves and enjoy some quick and dirty sex."

The construction worker then asks the handyman what he would do to which he replies, "I'm going to keep perfectly still."

The Sexy Housewife

A handyman was called out to repair a squeaky door.

The woman who invited him was incredibly sexy and a bit flirty. After the handyman had finished she paid him and said, "I'm going to make a request to you. It's embarrassing to talk about, but while my husband is a kind, decent man - sigh - he has a certain physical weakness. Now, I'm a woman and you're a strong man."

The repairman was finding it hard to control himself "Yes, I am sure I am able to help you out. What exactly would you like me to do?" he said.

She said "I've been wanting to ask you ever since you came in the door."

The handyman quivered, "Yes, Yes."

The woman then asked, "Would you please help me move the refrigerator?"

The Best Way to Pray

A vicar and a minister were in the vicarage discussing the best positions for prayer while a handyman worked on repairing one of the vicars' kitchen cupboards.

The vicar said, "Kneeling is definitely the best way to pray."

The minister said, "I find I get the best results when I am standing with my hands outstretched to Heaven."

The repairman told them, "The best praying I have ever done was when I was hanging upside down from a ladder."

The Parrot and the Handyman

A handyman is called to the house of a cute little old lady to fix her tumble dryer. There is a restless Doberman sitting in the kitchen growling under his breath at him, and also in the room is a parrot whistling happily in his cage.

Half-way through the job, the little old lady tells him she's going to the grocery store. The handyman asks the little old lady if he'll be safe while she's away to which she smiles and says: "Oh yes. Poopsie is so sweet. He wouldn't hurt a fly. But do not say anything at all to the parrot!"

Sure enough the dog ignored the handyman but the parrot starts to make horrible noises and is calling the handyman all manner of rude names.

The handyman finds it hard to work and yells at the bird: "Shut up, you feathered fruitcake."

The bird is stunned into silence.

A few seconds later, the parrot squawks: "Stick it to him, Poopsie!"

Take Two

A young boy was watching a handyman working on the upper story of a house. He saw the handyman drop a hammer, and saw him climb down the ladder to retrieve it.

The boy tells him, "My daddy would have two hammers so he wouldn't have to climb the ladder when he dropped one."

The handyman climbs back up the ladder and returns to work. Within a few minutes, he drops his screwdriver, and climbs back down the ladder.

The boy tells him, "My daddy would have two screwdrivers so he wouldn't have to climb down the ladder when he dropped one."

A little while later, the handyman has to go to the bathroom. Unfortunately, he has no way of getting inside the house, so he climbs down the ladder and relieves himself behind a bush.

As he is finishing up, he notices that the little boy has followed him and he asked the lad, "Well, I suppose your daddy has two of these too?"

"No," says the boy, "but my daddy's is twice as big."

Pulling Power

Carlo the property developer and his handyman buddy John, went bar-hopping every week together, and every week Carlo would go home with a hot woman while John went home alone.

One week John asked Carlo his secret to picking up women. "That's easy," said Carlo "When she asks you what you do for a living, don't tell her you're a handyman. Tell her you're a lawyer."

Later John is dancing with a hot woman when she leans in and asks him what he does for a living.

"I'm a lawyer," says John. The woman smiles and asks, "Want to go back to my place? It's just around the corner."

So, they go to her place, have some fun and an hour later, John is back in the bar telling Carlo about his success.

"I've only been a lawyer for an hour," John tittered, "And I've already screwed someone!"

Train Noise

A couple lives nearby some train tracks and it makes a thundering noise when it passes. The woman and her husband had to sleep with ear plugs in and they had to make the best of the situation since it was the only place they could afford.

Their closet door sat in such a way that when a train passed, the door would wobble in its sliders and by the time the train had passed, the door would be fully open.

One day, when her husband was at work, she decided to call a handyman to look at it.

He soon arrived and observed the effect when a train passes, but he isn't sure what causes it or what modifications the door needs so that it will stop wobbling open.

He decides to sit in the closet and wait for the next time it happens, to see if he can observe the cause. He doesn't really fit in the closet so he takes off his tool belt and leaves it outside the door.

The husband gets back home early and the wife greets him. However, he goes mad when he sees the handyman's boots in front of the bedroom, and his belt beside the closet.

He opens the closet to find the handyman and he demands, "Are you having an affair with my wife? What on earth are you doing in my closet?"

The handyman replies, "You won't believe this, but I'm waiting for a train."

Three Daughters

A handyman was talking to two of his buddies about their daughters.

The first friend says, "I was cleaning my daughter's room the other day and I found a pack of cigarettes. I didn't even know she smoked."

The second friend says, "That's nothing. I was cleaning my daughter's room the other day and I found an empty bottle of wine. I didn't even know she drank."

The handyman says, "That's nothing. I was cleaning my daughter's room the other day and I found a pack of condoms. I didn't even know she had a penis."

Lost Ear

A handyman is helping out his roofer buddy Gary for a week.

They are working on a house repairing some roof tiles.

Gary is up on the roof and accidentally cuts off his ear, and he yells down to his friend, "Hey - look out for my ear I just cut off."

The handyman looks around and calls up to Gary, "Is this your ear?"

Gary looks down and says "No. Mine had a pencil behind it!"

The Train Trip

Three handymen and three plumbers are about to board a train to a convention. As they were standing in line for tickets, the plumbers noticed that the handymen bought only one ticket between them.

The plumbers bought their three tickets and boarded the train but watched the handymen to see how they were going to manage with only one ticket.

As soon as the train left the station, the three handymen moved from their seats and they all squeezed into one restroom.

Soon the ticket collector passed through the carriage and knocked on the restroom door saying "Ticket please!" The door was opened slightly and an arm reached out and the one ticket was handed to the ticket collector.

The next day, the plumbers decided to do the same thing, so they only purchased one ticket between the three of them. However they noticed the handymen didn't purchase any tickets at all.

They all boarded the train and as soon as the train left the station, the three plumbers hurry for the restroom.

A few moments later, one of the handymen gets up from his seat, knocks on the restroom door and says, "Ticket please!"

The Frog

A 78 years old handyman was walking along the road one day when he came across a frog.

He reached down, picked the frog up, and started to put it in his pocket. As he did so, the frog said, "Kiss me on the lips and I'll turn into a beautiful woman, and make mad passionate love to you."

The old handyman continued to put the frog in his pocket when the frog said, "Didn't you hear what I said?"

The handyman looked at the frog and said, "Yes, but at my age I'd rather have a talking frog."

Chapter 6: Handyman Pick Up Lines

I am good at polishing things to make them nice and bright.

I've got a stripped screw – do you want to help me pry it loose?

Rest assured, I can unclog your septic tank.

I can use my snake to clean out your pipes.

I like hammering.

Can I hold your caulk?

You make me wetter than a new can of sealant.

You turn my two-by-four into a four-by-eight.

If I hook your cable up, will you hook mine up?

Your eyes are like wrenches. They make my nuts tighten.

I always wear my hard hat, baby.

I'm very good at tongue-and-groove work.

F*ck me if I'm wrong, but you want to screw me, don't you?

I know that you'd be able to screw my nuts.

You are the perfect switch. You turn me on.

Are you the secondary winding to my transformer, as I feel magnetically coupled to you.

Is there anything you'd like me to screw?

I know how to use my equipment.

I can hammer all day long.

Let's play carpenter. First we get hammered, I get some wood and then I nail you.

Chapter 7: Bumper Stickers for Handymen

Real men like sawdust.

Keep Calm and Call a Handyman.

There's no such thing as too many tools.

Eat, Sleep, Fix Stuff.
